flash and roar

Exploring the Science of Lightning and Thunder

sarah michaels

contents

So if you think of yourself as a bit like a weather detective, and you are trying to solve the mystery of what tomorrow's weather is going to be like, you would look at some clues. These clues would include how warm or cool the air will be for example (temperature), what the air would be doing (is the air moving? is it rising? is it falling?), and how wet it is (does the air contain a lot or a little moisture?). By understanding the clues you can work out whether or not you should take an umbrella with you to protect you from the rain or sunglasses to help you to see on a very sunny day.

preface

introduction to the book

Have you ever watched a big storm from your window? Have you ever wondered where the lightning comes from or what causes the thunder? Have you ever seen a lightning bolt and then tried to count to see how far away the thunder might be? If you've been standing at the window, watching the rain pour down, and wondering about the amazing weather outside, you've come to the right place!

This book will invite you into a world of storms—a world of howling winds, crashing waves, and flashing lightning. We will explore the science of weather to find out why these powerful and often beautiful displays of weather happen.

As you read, you'll find fun facts and new discoveries at every turn of the page! Let's pull out our equipment and prepare for the journey! First, we will head straight for the weather itself. Now, we all think we know what "weather" is. It's what the weatherman talks about on the radio. But weather is so much more than what he may describe on a daily time schedule. It's the wind blowing gently through the trees, the sunlight shining down on the picnic blanket, and the strong storms of winter.

So why not play the meteorologist? What if you could look at the sky, and then go inside and know whether to expect a storm, and how all those flashes and booms come about? It may sound like something that only adults have to do, but by the time you get to the end of this book you will be able to tell adults in your life lots of fun-facts about storms!

Lightning and thunder are not just awesome sights and sounds; they are also important pieces of a puzzle that helps people who study the Earth and learn about the atmosphere and the weather learn more about how they work! Lightning can move so fast that it almost does not seem possible and the sound of thunder can rumble and roll through the sky making a noise that can be heard very far away. It really is something to think about. That same shock you feel when you touch a doorknob after you shuffle your feet on a carpet because there is static electricity in your body is similar in a way to the giant spark that lightning makes when it comes to visit us.

While it is great fun to watch and to learn, it is also something you can try out for yourself! We've got all sorts of activities and experiments that you can try at home that will bring the magic of meteorology to you, safe and sound inside your house, and sometimes even just beyond the back door.

You can create a storm in a small container and watch the principles of weather in action. These activities are safe, a lot of fun, and a brilliant way to learn science through practical, hands-on experiments.

Then what about thunder? Have you ever rubbed a balloon between your hands to make it squeak or squeal? The same is true of thunder. When lightning causes the air to heat up very quickly, in the same way that you can heat up the air in a balloon by quickly moving your hands, it expands incredibly quickly and creates a loud noise - thunder!

We'll talk about why sometimes it's a deep, rumbling sound, and at other times the sound is a much sharper crack.

Along our journey we'll tell you some of the most amazing stories you will ever hear - stories of historic storms and the tremendous effects they have had on towns and cities. and explore the many myths and legends people have told about thunder and lightning over time. You might even want to write a stormy story of your own! As we look at lightning and thunder together, let me be your guide.

We won't just learn about the weather, but how to see the world in a whole new way. We'll understand how the pieces of our world fit together to create the weather we know. And who knows?

Maybe your weather knowledge will help you predict the weather on TV! Or maybe you'll be the one teaching kids about the secrets of the skies. So, pull on your galoshes and buckle up your curiosity, because it's time for the journey of a lifetime. Every page will bring new facts and fun, and by the end, you'll be a true storm expert. Are you ready?

Then let's go explore the magical world of lightning and thunder!

safety tips when reading about and exploring weather phenomena

Are you ready to become storm-chasing royalty? Before we start forecasting meteorological clouds or reenacting our favorite tornado scenes from the Wizard of Oz in our backyards, it's important that we learn to be both safe and aware. Weather can be fascinating and fun, but it also strikes adventure-seekers with unpredictable problems, and that's why it's so important to know how to be safe during various storm events.

So, first things first-made sure you're reading or watching about this storm event somewhere with someone, and not just out in this thing all willy nilly!

If it's a thunderstomring and you're at home, I can certainly assure you that it is pretty safe to be home and observe things going on in the sky-or if it's a super intense tornado, that is dangerous. Either way, knowing how to be safe is just as important as knowing why the weather changes, I think, so let's get started on the safety and danger of this storm chasing.

1. Understanding Weather Alerts

Do you know how to tell if bad weather is on the way? Weather alerts can be your best friend when it comes to staying safe. There are watches and warnings issued by weather services that can tell you what to expect. A 'watch' means that weather conditions are likely to happen, and you should keep an eye on the sky. A 'warning' means that the weather condition is already happening or will happen soon, and you should take action to stay safe. It's like getting a heads-up from a friend to finish your outdoor game and head home before the rain starts pouring.

2. The Safe Spots During a Storm

If you're at home and a storm is brewing, do you

know where the safest place is to go? Avoid windows, as they can shatter during strong wind gusts or from flying debris. Basements are great during tornadoes because they are below ground level, and the earth can provide extra protection from high winds. No basement? No problem! A small, windowless room or hallway on the lowest floor is also a good spot. Think of it as your mini fortress against the storm.

3. What If You're Outside?

Sometimes storms sneak up on us when we're playing outside. If the sky starts to look scary, it's time to head indoors. But what if you can't get inside right away? Avoid open fields and tall objects like trees and poles. These are favorites for lightning strikes. If you're caught in a wide-open space, crouch down with your heels touching and your head between your knees. Make yourself as small a target as possible for lightning.

4. Watching Weather Safely

Curious about how thunderstorms develop or what makes a hurricane? There's a safe way to watch these powerful natural events without being in harm's way. You can follow weather updates on TV or use apps that show live weather conditions. This way, you can watch the storm's progress from the safety of your home. Remember, never try to go out and take pictures of severe weather unless you're with an adult who knows it's safe.

5. Experimenting with Weather

Would you like to try some cool weather experiments? You can create a mini tornado with bottles or make a cloud in a jar. These experiments are safe to do at home and can help you understand how weather works. Always ask an adult to help you with experiments, especially if they involve using things like hot water or electricity.

6. Preparing for the Unexpected

Sometimes, despite our best plans, weather can surprise us. It's smart to have an emergency kit ready with items like water, snacks, a flashlight, and extra batteries. You can even make a checklist of things to include in your kit. This can be a fun project, and it will also make you feel like a weather-ready warrior!

7. Learning with Lightning

Lightning is fascinating, but it's also very dangerous. When you hear thunder, remember that lightning isn't far behind. If you're home, stay away from windows, doors, and electrical appliances. You can watch the lightning from a safe distance inside and count how long it takes to hear the thunder. This can help you figure out how far away the lightning is. Just remember, every five seconds between the lightning flash and the sound of thunder means the storm is about one mile away.

8. Staying Informed

One of the best safety tools is knowledge. The more you know about weather, the better prepared you'll be. Read books, watch educational shows about weather, and maybe even attend a weather workshop if there's one nearby. Knowledge is power, especially when it comes to understanding the forces of nature.

By knowing these safety tips, you can enjoy learning about the weather without worry. Whether you're reading about tornadoes, experimenting with static electricity, or watching a thunderstorm roll in, always remember that staying safe is your number one priority. Now, equipped with your new knowledge and safety tips, you're ready to tackle any storm that comes your way with confidence and curiosity. Let's keep exploring the sky, but always with safety in mind!

1 /
what is weather?

introduction to weather: what it is and why it matters

WHAT IS WEATHER EXACTLY? No need to bring an umbrella if you don't know the answer right off the bat, or wear shorts in the heat of summer, for that matter. In truth, weather goes way beyond making sure we're dressed appropriately each day. Weather has a huge influence on everything we do, from how we dress to what we eat to the health of our planet. Explore the world as you learn how each day's weather turns up something new for you to discover!

Weather is the state of the atmosphere at any given time and place. When people talk about weather, they are usually concerned with temperature, humidity, precipitation, cloudiness, brightness, visibility, wind, and atmospheric pressure. It's kind of like being a detective— each of these elements gives a clue about what the atmosphere is up to, and knowing how to read them can help us prepare for our day.

Temperature Tells a Story

· · ·

Think about the last time you checked the thermometer before heading out. Why do you think it's cooler in the morning and warmer in the afternoon? It's all about the sun! As the sun rises, it heats the earth, which in turn heats the air above it. This daily dance of heat is just one of the stories that temperature can tell us.

Rain: More Than Just Droplets

Rain is another key character in our weather story. It does more than just soak your socks; it's vital for all living things. Plants need rain to grow, and animals (including us!) need fresh water to drink. When clouds get heavy with water, they let it fall as rain, giving life to everything it touches.

But have you ever wondered why some places get more rain than others? Or why rain can feel like a sudden surprise? It's all about how warm air can hold more water than cool air. When warm, moist air rises and cools down, it releases that water as rain. Understanding this helps us predict when and where it might rain, and even prepare for floods when there's too much rain at once.

. . .

Winds of Change

Winds are more than just a cool breeze on a hot day. They're the Earth's way of balancing out heat. When warm air rises, cooler air rushes in to take its place, creating wind. Wind can tell us a lot about what's coming in the weather. For example, a sudden change in wind direction might mean a storm is coming.

The Power of Storms

Speaking of storms, they're some of the most dramatic parts of weather. From booming thunderstorms to whirling tornadoes and mighty hurricanes, these are the Earth's most powerful ways of releasing energy. Storms help balance out the temperature on Earth by moving heat from warm areas to cooler areas. But they can also be dangerous, so knowing about them is crucial for staying safe.

Why Weather Matters

· · ·

You might be thinking, "Why do we need to learn all this?" Well, weather affects everything! Farmers depend on weather to grow crops. Pilots need to know weather conditions to fly safely. Architects design buildings based on local weather, like making them stronger in places with lots of hurricanes or adding features to handle heavy snow.

And it's not just about today. Understanding weather helps us look into the future, too. By knowing how weather patterns affect the environment, we can make better choices to protect our planet. Things like using less energy, saving water, and planting trees can all help make a big difference in our climate.

Staying Weather-Smart

As you learn about weather, you'll start to see the signs nature gives us about what's going to happen next. Maybe you'll notice how the clouds are forming on your way to school and predict that it might rain later. Or you'll feel the wind change and guess that it might get cooler soon. Being weather-smart means you're always ready, no matter what the day brings.

. . .

Explorers of the Atmosphere

Every time you step outside, you're experiencing the atmosphere in action. The changes you feel and see from morning to night and from season to season are all part of Earth's amazing weather system. By understanding these patterns, you'll not only know what to wear or what activities are best for the day, but you'll also be more connected to the world around you.

Weather is a huge part of our lives, and the more we know about it, the better we can live and grow in harmony with our planet. So, keep your eyes on the sky and your mind ready to learn. Every cloud, wind, and raindrop has a story to tell, and you can be the one to tell it!

brief overview of different types of weather

As we continue our journey through the fascinating world of meteorology, let's take a closer look at the many different types of weather you might encounter, no matter where you are on the planet. Weather isn't just about sunny days and rainy afternoons; it's a rich tapestry that includes every type of atmosphere action you can imagine—and some you probably can't!

Sunshine and Clear Skies

Let's start with everyone's favorite: sunny weather. When the sky is clear, and the sun is shining, it often means high pressure is in control of the area. High pressure pushes air downward, preventing clouds from forming. Sunshine is fantastic for outdoor activities, helps plants grow, and even boosts our mood with a little natural vitamin D!

Clouds: Nature's Artwork

Clouds are more than just fluffy, floating mysteries. They come in all shapes, sizes, and altitudes, and each type tells us something about the weather. High, wispy cirrus clouds often mean good weather now but indicate a change could be coming. Thick, gray stratus clouds might bring drizzle and a gloomy day, while towering cumulonimbus clouds are the giants behind thunderstorms and heavy rainfalls.

Rain: More than Just Drops

Rain is essential for life, helping to fill our rivers, water our crops, and replenish the soil. But did you know there are different types of rain? Light, steady rain often comes from stratus clouds and might hang around all day, creating a perfect setting for reading or drawing inside. Heavy rain usually drops from cumulonimbus clouds and can come with a side of thunder and lightning.

Fog and Mist: The Mysterious Twins

Fog and mist are like weather's magicians. They create eerie scenes where everything looks mysterious. Fog happens when the ground cools down overnight and warm, moist air above it condenses into tiny water droplets. It's especially thick and can cover entire cities or just hover over rivers and lakes. Mist is lighter and often seen after rainfalls, giving the air a soft, dreamy quality.

. . .

Snow and Ice: The Winter Ballet

When temperatures drop, rain can turn into snow, sleet, or hail. Snowflakes are ice crystals that stick together, creating winter wonderlands. Each snowflake is unique, and under the right conditions, you can even catch them on your gloves and see their intricate designs. Sleet is rain that freezes as it falls, turning into ice pellets that bounce on the ground. Hail, however, forms in strong thunderstorms when updrafts of air keep pushing water droplets higher until they freeze.

Wind: The Invisible Mover

Wind is air in motion, moving from areas of high pressure to low pressure. It can be a gentle breeze that rustles the leaves or a howling gale that bends trees and whips up waves on the sea. Winds have names based on their strength, like gusts, breezes, squalls, and hurricanes.

. . .

Thunderstorms: The Sky's Drama

Thunderstorms are one of nature's most spectacular shows. They happen when warm, moist air rises quickly in the atmosphere, cooling and condensing to form a storm cloud. Inside these clouds, electrical charges build up until they're released as lightning, which causes the thunder we hear. Thunderstorms can bring heavy rains, strong winds, and sometimes even hail.

Hurricanes and Tornadoes: The Big Spinners

These are the heavyweights of weather. Hurricanes form over warm ocean waters and can pack winds of over 74 miles per hour, bringing heavy rain and huge waves. They can be massive, affecting entire regions. Tornadoes are more localized but incredibly powerful, with the fastest winds on earth. They form during severe thunderstorms and can rip buildings apart and toss cars around as if they were toys.

introduction to storms as a weather phenomenon

Now that we've journeyed through the various types of weather, let's dive into one of nature's most exhilarating phenomena—storms. Storms can be thrilling and dramatic, showcasing the power of our atmosphere in full force. They can bring rain, lightning, wind, and sometimes snow or hail. But what exactly makes a storm, and why do they happen? Let's find out together!

What Makes a Storm?

A storm is a disturbance in the Earth's atmosphere that involves sudden changes in air pressure and usually includes strong winds. It often also involves precipitation like rain, hail, or snow. To understand storms, think of the atmosphere as a giant sea of air that's always moving and changing. When different parts of this "air ocean" collide, a storm can form.

The Ingredients of a Storm

. . .

Storms need three main ingredients: moisture, unstable air, and lift. Moisture in the air is what forms clouds and rain. Unstable air means warm air that can rise rapidly. Lift is what pushes the air up, which could be heat from the earth, mountains that air flows over, or fronts where two different air masses meet.

Types of Storms

There are many types of storms, each with its own unique features. Let's look at a few:

1. Thunderstorms - These occur when moist air rises quickly into the atmosphere, forming tall, dense clouds known as cumulonimbus clouds. The energy from the rising moisture creates lightning and thunder. Thunderstorms are famous for their intensity and can also bring torrential rain, hail, and gusty winds.

2. Tornadoes - These are violent storms that form under very specific conditions: during severe thunderstorms, when there's a lot of wind shear and instability in the atmosphere. Tornadoes are rapidly spinning columns of

air that touch the ground, and they can cause tremendous destruction in a very short time.

3. Hurricanes - Known in different parts of the world as typhoons or cyclones, these massive storm systems form over warm ocean waters and can have winds of over 74 miles per hour. They gain energy from the warm waters and can grow large and powerful, affecting vast areas with high winds, heavy rain, and flooding.

4. Blizzards - These are severe snowstorms with very strong winds and intense snowfall. Visibility during a blizzard can be very low, and the conditions can make travel and being outdoors extremely dangerous.

Why Do Storms Matter?

You might wonder why we need to learn about storms if they seem so scary. Well, storms are a crucial part of our world's weather system. They help distribute heat and moisture around the planet, which helps regulate our climate. Also, the rain from storms is vital for filling rivers and watering crops.

. . .

Watching Storms Safely

While storms can be exciting to watch, it's super important to do it safely. Watching a storm from a secure place inside, like your home or school, can be a fantastic way to learn. You can see how the storm develops, how the wind behaves, and how quickly the weather can change. Just make sure you stay away from windows and doors to avoid any surprises from sudden gusts or lightning.

Storm Chasers: The Bold Explorers

Did you know there are scientists called storm chasers? They use special equipment to go safely near storms to study them. They learn how storms form and behave, which helps weather forecasters predict storms more accurately and give better warnings to keep people safe.

Learning from Storms

. . .

Every storm can teach us something new about our planet's complex weather systems. By studying storms, scientists have learned how to better predict not just storms but other weather conditions too. This helps everyone from farmers planning their crops to families planning their vacations.

2 /
the story of lightning

what is lightning?

HAVE you ever watched a thunderstorm and seen the sky illuminated by bright lines of light? This is lightning, nature's own light machine! Lightning is not just a fun show of light; it is in fact a massive natural electric shock. Let's wire our way into the electric universe as we learn all about lightning!

The Spark of Electricity in the Sky

Lightning is a sudden, electrical discharge that occurs during a thunderstorm. This discharge is nature's way of balancing out the electrical charge between the clouds and the ground, or between different clouds. Imagine the sky is filled with energy, like a charged-up battery, and when it gets too full, it needs to release some of that energy. That release is what we see as lightning!

How Does Lightning Form?

The story of lightning starts with the storm clouds, called cumulonimbus clouds, which are the thunderstorm clouds. They are the tall, anvil-shaped clouds you can see for miles away depending on how big the storm is. Inside the clouds, there are little droplets and ice particles that are bashing into each other because of the strong updrafts and downdrafts that are in the cloud.

So, all this stuff bashing into each other creates the charge that's carried to the cloud because of the wind. And after a little bit, the charge gets separated: the top of the cloud becomes positive, the bottom of the cloud becomes negative, and this creates an electric field within the storm cloud, and also between the cloud and the ground. When the electric field gets strong enough, then we have lightning, and the electric field needs to be neutralized.

The Journey of a Lightning Bolt

The process begins when a step leader, a channel of negatively charged electricity, is formed by the cloud and seems to shoot down towards the ground. The leader, which is invisible to the human eye, is itself composed of a series smaller stepping pulses and moves in a jagged, step-like path. As the step leader closes in on the ground, the ground releases positively charged energy.

As a result, an electrical bridge is formed between the leader and the ground and a powerful spark known as the return stroke follows. This event is what we actually see as lightning. The flash that we see is the return stroke in which the charges are neutralized and energy is discharged back up into the cloud. All this occurs in only a fraction of a second which is why that spark appears so sudden and strong.

Different Types of Lightning

- Cloud-to-Ground Lightning: This is the type most of us think of when we imagine lightning. It's what happens when electric charges travel between the cloud and the earth, creating a spectacular light show.

- Cloud-to-Cloud Lightning: Sometimes the electric charges travel between different clouds. This type of lightning can also be very bright and is usually more horizontal.

- Intra-cloud Lightning: This occurs within a single cloud and is the most common type of lightning. It might be harder to see because it's often obscured by other clouds.

Lightning Safety

While lightning is fascinating to watch, it's also extremely powerful and can be dangerous. It's important to stay safe during a thunderstorm:

- If you're outside and hear thunder, find a safe indoor place immediately.

- Stay away from tall objects like trees and poles which can attract lightning.
- Inside the house, avoid using wired electronics and stay away from windows, as glass can shatter if lightning strikes nearby.

Learning and Observing Safely

You can learn about lightning from the safety of your home by watching documentaries or using online resources that explain more about weather phenomena. Some scientists use high-speed cameras to study lightning, capturing images that show the formation of the bolt in incredible detail. These can provide a closer look at how lightning works without any risk.

Lightning in Culture

Throughout history, people have been in awe of lightning, and it has appeared in many myths and legends. In ancient Greek mythology, Zeus, the king of the gods, was said to wield lightning bolts as his weapon. This shows just how powerful and important lightning has been in human culture and imagination.

how does lightning form? (simple explanation of the build-up of electrical charges)

Ever wonder how lightning comes to life in our skies? It's like a magic trick that nature pulls off, but once you learn how it's done, you'll see it's all part of a fascinating scientific process. Let's break down how lightning really forms, step by electrifying step.

A Storm Brews

Our story begins in a storm cloud, also known as a cumulonimbus cloud. These are the big, towering clouds that often signal a thunderstorm is on the way. Inside these clouds, there's a lot happening that sets the stage for lightning.

Charging Up the Cloud

. . .

Within the storm cloud, there are tons of tiny ice crystals and water droplets moving around in the air. These particles move very quickly, especially when the wind is strong up there in the cloud. As they move and bump into each other, something really interesting happens— they start to exchange electrical charges.

Think of it like when you shuffle your feet on a carpet and then touch a doorknob and feel a shock. That shock is because of the build-up of static electricity, which is pretty much what's happening in the cloud but on a much, much larger scale.

Separating the Charges

In the cloud, as these ice crystals and droplets continue to crash into each other, they start sorting themselves out by charge. The heavier, negatively charged particles tend to sink to the bottom of the cloud, while the lighter, positively charged particles tend to rise to the top. This separation creates a powerful electric field within the cloud and between the cloud and the ground.

. . .

The Electric Field Grows

This electric field grows stronger and stronger as the charges build up. If you could see it, it might look like a stretching rubber band, getting tighter and tighter. The electric field is just waiting for a chance to snap—that snap is what we see as lightning.

Stepping Down

As the electric field becomes incredibly strong, a leader of electricity (called a stepped leader because it steps down from the cloud in stages) starts its journey toward the Earth. This leader is invisible to us at first because it's not yet bright or carrying enough charge to glow. It moves in steps, coming closer and closer to the ground, seeking out a path of least resistance.

Answering the Call

Meanwhile, the ground beneath the storm cloud isn't just sitting there; it's reacting to the electric field.

Objects on the ground that are good conductors of electricity, like tall buildings, trees, or even the ground itself, start sending up positive charges toward the cloud in a process called streamer formation. These streamers rise up, trying to meet the stepped leader coming down.

The Connection

When a stepped leader and a streamer finally meet, the path is completed, and a strong electrical current flows. This current zaps down the path created by the leader in a brilliant flash of light—this is the lightning bolt that we see. The whole process happens in the blink of an eye, lighting up the sky and sometimes startling us with its sudden brilliance.

The Thunderous Applause

After the lightning bolt flashes, we hear thunder. That's because the lightning heats the air around it so fast that the air expands explosively, creating a sound wave that we hear as thunder. It's like nature's applause for the incredible electrical performance we just witnessed in the sky!

Lightning Across the Globe

Lightning isn't just an occasional show; it happens all the time, all over the world. About 44 times every second, somewhere around the globe, a lightning bolt is hitting the ground. That's a lot of electricity!

Why It Matters

Understanding how lightning forms helps us appreciate this powerful natural phenomenon and teaches us about the incredible energy systems of our planet. It also helps scientists predict when and where thunderstorms will occur, making it easier to keep people safe by warning them about severe weather.

types of lightning (cloud-to-ground, cloud-to-cloud, etc.)

Have you ever marveled at a lightning storm and wondered if all lightning is the same? Well, strap in, because we're about to dive into the electrifying world of lightning types. Each kind of lightning has its own unique characteristics and secrets, and understanding them can be as exciting as watching a live lightning show!

The Sparkling Spectrum of Lightning

Lightning may look similar at first glance, but there are several distinct types, each with its own way of traveling through the sky. Let's explore these fascinating varieties:

1. Cloud-to-Ground Lightning (CG)

   - This is the type you probably think of when you imagine lightning. It's the most dramatic and easily observed form. Cloud-to-ground lightning happens when a channel of negative charge, called a stepped leader, descends from the cloud toward the earth. It is met by a streamer, a channel of positive charge that reaches up from the ground. When they connect, zap! Energy flows, and we see the lightning bolt flash across the sky.

- Cloud-to-ground lightning is responsible for those big, bright bolts that seem to split the sky. It can be dangerous because it can strike objects on the ground, like trees, buildings, or even people if they're not in safe places during a storm.

2. Cloud-to-Cloud Lightning (CC)

- Also known as intercloud or sheet lightning, cloud-to-cloud lightning occurs between different cloud areas. It might happen between different parts of the same cloud or between two separate clouds. This type is more common than cloud-to-ground and often lights up an entire cloud, giving it a glowing appearance.

- Cloud-to-cloud lightning shows us the vast energy exchanges that happen high in the sky, mostly unseen from the ground. It's spectacular to watch, especially at night, because it can illuminate large sections of the sky with a ghostly light.

3. Intra-cloud Lightning (IC)

- The most frequent type of lightning, intra-cloud lightning, occurs within a single cloud. This happens when different areas of positive and negative charges within the cloud interact with each other, creating a lightning bolt that travels inside the cloud.

- Intra-cloud lightning might not always be visible to us on the ground, as it can be hidden by dense cloud cover. However, it contributes to the overall illumination of the cloud during a storm, adding to the majestic display of a thunderstorm.

4. Anvil Crawlers

- These are a type of cloud-to-cloud lightning that is fascinating to watch. They spread across the sky along the top of the cloud, often branching out like tree limbs. Anvil crawlers are named for their slow, crawling appearance and they light up vast areas of the sky as they travel.

- Anvil crawlers are often seen with severe thunderstorms and can be a sign that the storm is particularly strong and charged.

5. Positive Lightning

- While most lightning carries a negative charge from the cloud to the ground, positive lightning is different. It occurs when a positive charge from the upper levels of a cloud strikes down. This type of lightning is less common, but it's far more powerful and can strike further away from the main storm cloud, catching observers by surprise.

- Positive lightning is particularly dangerous because of its power and the long distance it can cover. It can strike out of what seems like a clear sky, which is why it's also called a "bolt from the blue."

Watching Lightning Safely

Now that you know about the different types of lightning, it's important to remember to watch them safely. Lightning is beautiful but also extremely power-ful. Always stay indoors during a thunderstorm, away from windows, and never use wired electronics. Observing lightning can be thrilling, but your safety is the most important thing.

3 /
thunder rolls

what causes thunder?

HAVE you ever thought about how far away a storm is by counting the seconds between the flash of lightning and the clap of thunder? That's a fun way to put science to the test if ever I have seen one.

Real-life science experiments are the best kind, don't you think? During our last meeting, we were caught up in awe at lightning. Now, get ready to hear about the rumble that comes after the light show by tuning into thunder. So, what is thunder anyway, and why do we hear it after lightning? Welcome to the wonderful world of noise, otherwise known as thunder.

The Sound of Energy

Thunder is the sound that comes from the sudden expansion of air around a lightning bolt. When lightning strikes, it heats the air around it incredibly quickly—faster than you can blink! This air gets so hot so fast that it doesn't just get warm; it explodes outward because it has to make room for how much bigger it's gotten. This explosion of expanding air creates a sound wave that we hear as thunder.

. . .

How Hot? Super Hot!

To understand just how hot lightning is, imagine this: The air around a lightning bolt can heat up to about 54,000 degrees Fahrenheit (that's about 30,000 degrees Celsius). That's hotter than the surface of the sun! When something gets that hot that fast, the air around it expands explosively. This rapid expansion sends shock waves through the air, similar to a sonic boom.

Crack or Rumble: The Sound of Thunder

Have you noticed that not all thunder sounds the same? Sometimes it's a sharp crack, and other times it's a long, rumbling growl. Why the difference? Well, it all depends on how far away and how the lightning bolt travels through the sky.

- Sharp Cracks: These are usually heard when lightning is close by. The sound doesn't have much time to bounce around or get absorbed by the environment, so it reaches your ears quickly and sounds like a sharp snap.
    - Long Rumbles: When thunder rumbles, it's because

the lightning bolt might be traveling far away from you, and it might be zigzagging through the clouds. The sound waves bounce off clouds and hills, and some parts of the thunder sound reach you later than others, making it seem like it's lasting a long time.

Echoes in the Atmosphere

Another cool thing about thunder is how it can echo off landscapes like mountains, buildings, and large water bodies. If you're in a city with lots of tall buildings, thunder can bounce off multiple surfaces and create a series of echoes, making the thunder last longer and sound more dramatic.

The Speed of Sound

Sound travels at a speed of about 340 meters per second (about 1,115 feet per second). That's pretty fast, but light travels much faster—that's why we see lightning before we hear the thunder. By counting the seconds between seeing lightning and hearing thunder, you can roughly calculate how far away the storm is. Every five seconds you count means the storm is about one mile away. This little trick is a fun way to play meteorologist at home!

Thunder Safety

While thunder itself isn't harmful, it tells us that lightning is nearby, which is dangerous. A good rule to remember is, "When thunder roars, go indoors." This means if you can hear thunder, even if it's not very loud, you are within range of where the next lightning strike could occur. It's best to stay safe inside until the storm passes.

Learning from Thunder

Every clap of thunder can teach us something about the storm it comes from. Scientists use the sound of thunder to help understand the lightning it followed and to study how storms develop. By listening to and studying different kinds of thunder sounds, scientists can learn a lot about the energy and distance of lightning in a storm.

· · ·

Thunder in Stories and Culture

Across different cultures and throughout history, thunder has played a big role in stories and mythology. Many cultures saw thunder as the voice of powerful gods controlling the weather. These stories helped people make sense of the powerful, often scary sounds that thunderstorms can bring.

explaining the relationship between lightning and thunder

Have you ever watched a dramatic thunderstorm with flashes of lightning followed by big booms of thunder and wondered how these two spectacular events are related? Well, you're in for a treat! Today, we're going to unravel the exciting connection between lightning and thunder, two of nature's most thrilling displays.

Lightning Strikes and Thunder Rolls

Lightning and thunder are inseparable buddies in the world of weather. They always appear together during a thunderstorm, but have you noticed that we always see the lightning before we hear the thunder? Let's discover why that happens!

The Birth of Lightning

Let's look at how lightning is made. In a storm cloud, there are countless small ice crystals and water droplets moving about. As they get blown around, they often collide, generating an electric charge. After some time, the cloud is filled with so much electric energy that it becomes overloaded. It has too many positive charges at its top and too many negative charges at the bottom. So, a lightning bolt shoots out to resolve the situation. Lightning can fork out completely within a single cloud, from one cloud to another, or from a cloud to the ground.

The Spark Heats the Air

When lightning flashes, it heats the air around it in a flash—literally! The air can heat up to about 54,000 degrees Fahrenheit, which is hotter than the surface of the sun. When something gets this hot this fast, it expands explosively. This sudden expansion of air creates a shock wave.

· · ·

From Shock Wave to Sound Wave

This shock wave moves through the air, spreading out from the path of the lightning bolt. As it moves, it cools down and turns into a sound wave that we hear as thunder. The process is a bit like popping a balloon. Imagine the air inside the balloon pushing out quickly when the balloon bursts—that's similar to the shock wave created by the heated air.

Why the Delay?

Now, why do we see lightning before we hear thunder? It's all about the speed of light and sound. Light travels much faster than sound. The light from the lightning travels to your eyes almost instantly, so you see the lightning as soon as it happens. But sound waves (thunder) travel much slower, so it takes longer for the sound to reach your ears. Depending on how far away you are from the lightning, it might be a few seconds or even longer before you hear the thunder.

Counting the Seconds

. . .

You can actually use this delay to figure out how far away the lightning is. When you see a flash of lightning, start counting the seconds until you hear the thunder. Every five seconds you count equals about one mile distance from where the lightning struck. This little trick turns you into a live-action weather scientist, right from your own window!

Different Thunder Sounds

Not all thunder sounds the same. Close lightning strikes might make a sharp, loud crack because the sound wave is short and intense. Farther away, the thunder might rumble because the sound wave has more time to echo and bounce through the atmosphere before it reaches you. The shape of the landscape, like mountains and buildings, can also change how thunder sounds.

Thunder in Cultures Around the World

. . .

Across different cultures and ages, people have been fascinated by lightning and thunder. Many cultures thought of thunder as the voice of powerful gods. These stories and myths show just how important and impressive thunder and lightning have been to people all over the world for centuries.

Keep Exploring

Now that you know how lightning and thunder work together to create one of nature's most awesome shows, you can appreciate the next storm with a new understanding of what's going on up in the sky. Every storm is a chance to see science in action, with electricity, light, and sound all playing their parts in the thrilling drama of weather.

The Science of Sound and Light

Remember, lightning and thunder occur at the same time during a storm, but light travels much faster than sound. That's why we see lightning almost immediately, but we hear the thunder later. This difference can actually help us figure out how far away the lightning is, and knowing this is key to staying safe.

Counting the Gap

When you see a flash of lightning, start counting the seconds until you hear the thunder. You can count quickly, like this: one-Mississippi, two-Mississippi, three-Mississippi, and so on. For every five seconds you count, the lightning is about one mile away. This is called the "flash-to-bang" method. If you count to five (one-Mississippi to five-Mississippi), the lightning is one mile away; if you count to 10, it's two miles away, and so on.

What Does This Tell Us About Safety?

Meteorologists—the scientists who study the weather—tell us that if you can hear thunder, you are close enough to be struck by lightning. This rule helps us understand that thunderstorms are dangerous even when they seem to be far away. Lightning can travel sideways for many miles from the storm cloud before it strikes the ground, in what is sometimes called a "bolt from the blue."

. . .

The 30-30 Rule for Safety

To keep safe, weather experts recommend the 30-30 Rule:

- 30 Seconds: If the time between seeing lightning and hearing thunder is 30 seconds or less, the lightning is close enough to be a threat. That's about six miles away or less.

- 30 Minutes: After the last flash of lightning, wait at least 30 minutes before going outside again. This gives the storm enough time to move away and reduces the risk of being struck by a late bolt of lightning.

Why Keeping Distance Matters

Lightning is both fascinating and deadly. It can carry up to one billion volts of electricity in a single strike! That's enough power to light up a whole town for a moment. Because it's so powerful, lightning can cause serious injuries or even be fatal. Understanding how to gauge its distance helps us find a safe place when a storm hits.

. . .

Finding Shelter: The Safest Spots

When you hear thunder, it's best to move indoors. A building with wiring and plumbing is the safest place because if lightning strikes, it can travel through the wires and pipes into the ground, keeping you safe. Here are some tips for staying safe indoors:

- Stay away from windows, doors, and anything that connects to the outside like televisions, sinks, tubs, and corded phones.

- If you can't get to a building, a car with a metal top and sides is a good second choice. Just make sure all the windows are closed!

Outdoor Safety: When You Can't Get Inside

Sometimes, you might get caught outside when a storm rolls in. If you can't get to a safe building or car, avoid open fields, the tops of hills, and any tall objects like trees or poles. These places can attract lightning. Instead, find a low spot to wait out the storm. Crouch down on the balls of your feet, keep your head down, and cover your ears to protect against thunder.

• • •

Learning from Every Storm

Each thunderstorm gives us a chance to practice these safety tips. By understanding the relationship between lightning and thunder, and knowing how to measure the distance of a storm, you're becoming a smart, safe observer of nature's power.

Curiosity and Caution

As you continue to explore the wonders of weather, remember that your safety is the most important thing. Use your knowledge to enjoy watching storms without taking unnecessary risks. And the next time a storm approaches, impress your family and friends with your ability to gauge the distance of lightning using just the sound of thunder!

4 /
lightning safety

safety tips during thunderstorms

1. When Thunder Roars, Go Indoors!

This is the golden rule of thunderstorm safety. Lightning is beautiful to watch but extremely dangerous. If you hear thunder, even if it's faint, that means lightning is close enough to pose a risk. The safest place to be during a thunderstorm is indoors, away from windows, doors, and anything that could conduct electricity.

2. Avoid Electrical Equipment and Plumbing

Once you're safely inside, stay away from electrical appliances and fixtures, including corded telephones, computers, and gaming systems. Lightning can travel through electrical systems and phone lines. Water conducts electricity too, so avoid baths, showers, and washing dishes during a storm. It's better to wait until the storm passes before hopping into the shower or finishing those chores.

3. Windows and Doors: Keep Them Closed

It might be tempting to watch the storm from a window, but it's safer to stay away from all windows and doors. Lightning can break windows, and strong winds can send debris flying—both can be dangerous if you're too close. Find a comfy spot in the center of your house, maybe a hallway or a bathroom without windows, where you can listen to the storm safely.

4. If You're Caught Outside

Sometimes, despite our best plans, we might find ourselves outside when a storm hits. If you can't get to a safe indoor place quickly, avoid open fields, hilltops, and tall, isolated trees. These places can attract lightning. If you're in a forest, stay near lower trees. If you're in an open area, crouch down with your heels touching and your head down, but never lie flat on the ground—minimize your contact with the ground to reduce the risk of getting struck by lightning.

5. Cars as Safe Havens

If you're caught outside and there's no building to run to, your car can be a safe place. A car with a metal roof and the windows closed can provide protection. The metal frame of the vehicle can help direct the lightning around you and into the ground. Just avoid touching metal parts of the car during the storm.

6. Prepare Your Home

Before storm season hits, it's a good idea to prepare your home. Trim trees that could fall on your house, secure loose items in your yard that could become projectiles in strong winds, and make sure your roof and windows are in good shape to withstand heavy rain and wind.

7. Have an Emergency Kit Ready

It's smart to have an emergency kit in your home, especially in areas where storms are frequent. Your kit should include things like water, non-perishable food, a flashlight, extra batteries, a first-aid kit, and a portable charger for your cellphone. That way, if the power goes out, you'll have what you need to stay comfortable until it comes back on.

8. Listen to Weather Alerts

Stay informed about the weather by listening to weather forecasts, especially if you have plans to be outdoors. Weather apps on smartphones or a weather radio can alert you about severe thunderstorm warnings and watches. Knowing what to expect can help you stay safe by making smart decisions about where to be during a storm.

9. Educate Your Family

Make sure everyone in your family knows what to do if a thunderstorm hits. Have a family meeting to discuss your emergency plan, where to find the emergency kit, and what each person should do if caught outside during a storm. Practice going to your safe place at home so even the youngest family members know where to go.

Learning and Teaching

Understanding why these safety tips are important not only keeps you safe but also makes you a savvy science learner. Each rule is based on how thunderstorms work, from the electricity in lightning to the behavior of wind and rain. By following these tips, you're applying science to protect yourself and your loved ones.

what to do if you're outside or inside during a storm

If You're Inside During a Storm

Being inside is the safest place to be during a storm, but there are still some important steps to follow to keep safe:

1. Stay Away from Windows, Doors, and Porches: You might be tempted to watch the storm, but it's safer to stay away from windows, which could shatter during a storm from high winds or lightning strikes. Stay in interior rooms where you are protected from glass and other debris.

2. Unplug Electrical Devices: Protect your electronics and reduce the risk of power surges by unplugging TVs, computers, and other devices. Lightning can send a surge of power through electrical systems that might damage them.

3. Avoid Using Corded Phones and Appliances: Lightning can travel through plumbing and electrical systems. It's safe to use cell phones that aren't plugged into chargers, but avoid using landlines unless it's an emergency.

4. Stay Out of the Bath and Shower: Since lightning

can travel through pipes, it's a good idea to avoid taking a bath or shower during a thunderstorm. Wait until the storm passes before hopping into the tub or taking a shower.

5. Keep Doors and Windows Closed: This might seem obvious, but keeping windows and doors shut helps prevent strong winds and rain from entering your home, which can cause damage and injury.

If You Find Yourself Outside During a Storm

Sometimes you might get caught outside when a storm hits. Here's what to do if you can't get indoors immediately:

1. Avoid Open Fields and High Places: Lightning tends to strike the tallest object in an area. Avoid open fields and hilltops, and don't be the tallest object standing in an open area.

2. Stay Away from Tall Isolated Trees: It might seem like a good idea to take shelter under a tree, but it's actually one of the riskier places to be. If lightning strikes the tree, the electrical charge can jump to you, which is very dangerous.

3. Avoid Water: Stay out of pools, lakes, and other bodies of water. Water conducts electricity, so swimming during a thunderstorm is very risky.

4. Get Low, But Don't Lie Down: If you're caught in an open area, crouch down with your feet together, tuck your head, and cover your ears. However, don't lie flat

on the ground, as this increases your risk of being affected by electrical charges from a nearby lightning strike.

5. Keep Away from Metal Objects: Avoid fences, poles, and other metal objects, which can conduct electricity. Also, put down metal backpacks or other gear.

Cars as Safe Shelters

If a building isn't available, a fully enclosed, metal-topped vehicle can be a safe shelter. Close all the windows and avoid touching any metal surfaces. Here's why cars can be safe during a storm:

- Act Like a Faraday Cage: The metal frame of a car acts as a conductor. If lightning strikes the vehicle, the electricity will travel along the exterior metal body and into the ground without entering the interior.

Post-Storm Safety Tips

Once the storm has passed, there are still safety measures to keep in mind:

1. Wait for All Clear: Just because the rain stops doesn't mean the danger is over. Wait at least 30 minutes after the last clap of thunder before going outside again. This ensures the storm has truly moved away.

2. Check for Damage: If it's safe to do so, check around your home for any damage caused by the storm. Look for potential hazards like fallen wires or damaged electrical equipment. Don't touch any downed wires; instead, report them to local authorities.

3. Help Others: Check on neighbors, especially the elderly, who might need help or might not be aware of the damage.

Learning from Each Storm

Every storm gives us a chance to practice being safe and smart. By remembering these tips, you'll be better prepared for the next time a storm rolls in. Keep track of your experiences, and you'll become more knowledgeable about storm safety with each thunder clap and lightning flash.

Share Your Knowledge

Being storm-smart isn't just about keeping yourself safe; it's also about sharing what you know with friends and family. Teach others the safety tips you've learned, so they too can stay safe during storms. Maybe you can even create a storm safety drill at home or in school to practice what to do if a storm hits.

Stay Curious, Stay Prepared

Understanding what to do during storms is part of being a true weather enthusiast. Each storm can be different, so keep watching the skies and learning all you can about these amazing natural events. Remember, the more you know about storms, the better you can enjoy their beauty and power safely.

Keep exploring, keep learning, and always respect the power of nature. By being prepared and cautious, you can enjoy many more storm-watching adventures.

Let's keep our eyes on the clouds, our brains full of knowledge, and our spirits ready for the next weather adventure!

myths vs. facts about lightning safety

Hey there, young storm sleuths! Lightning is one of nature's most powerful displays, and with it comes a lot of myths and misunderstandings about how to stay safe. It's super important to know the difference between what's true and what's just a tall tale when it comes to lightning safety. Let's zap some common myths with the bright light of facts and keep you safe during the next storm!

Myth 1: It's safe to stand under a tree during a thunderstorm.

Fact: This might be one of the most dangerous myths out there! Trees are often struck by lightning because they are tall and isolated objects. If you stand under a tree, there's a risk that lightning could strike the tree and the electric current could jump to you, or the tree might fall over from the impact. Always avoid trees and seek a safer shelter, like a building or a car.

Myth 2: If it's not raining, there's no risk of lightning.

Fact: Lightning can strike out of the blue, literally! It can travel sideways for many miles from a distant storm and hit the ground on a clear day. This type of lightning strike is more rare but can be just as dangerous. That's why it's important to go indoors if you hear thunder, even if the sky above you looks clear and blue.

Myth 3: Wearing metal objects like jewelry or belts attracts lightning.

Fact: The presence of metal objects on your body doesn't make you more likely to be struck by lightning. However, metal does conduct electricity, so if lightning strikes nearby, metal can transmit the electricity to you. The best advice is to avoid large metal structures like fences or poles, which can conduct electricity from a strike.

Myth 4: Lying flat on the ground makes you safer during a lightning storm.

Fact: Lying flat increases your risk of being affected by potentially deadly ground current if lightning strikes the earth near you. If you're caught outside with no possible shelter, crouch down on the balls of your feet, put your hands over your ears to protect from thunder, and keep your head down. Make yourself as small a target as possible and minimize your contact with the ground.

Myth 5: If you're inside a house, you don't need to take any precautions.

Fact: While being inside a building significantly increases your safety during a storm, there are still precautions you should take. Avoid any contact with water, such as bathing or washing dishes, because plumbing can conduct electricity. Also, stay away from windows and doors, and don't use corded phones, as electrical wires can carry the electric charge from lightning.

Myth 6: Rubber tires on a car protect you from lightning by insulating you.

Fact: It's not the rubber tires that protect you in a car; it's the metal frame of the vehicle. When lightning strikes a vehicle, it is the metal frame that conducts the electrical charge around the occupants and safely into the ground. Always keep the windows closed and avoid touching metal components during a thunderstorm.

Myth 7: Lightning never strikes the same place twice.

Fact: Lightning can strike any location more than once, and places that are high or pointed can be struck multiple times during the same storm. For example, the Empire State Building is hit by lightning around 23 times a year.

Staying Informed and Safe

Knowing the facts about lightning and thunderstorms can help you make smart decisions about where to go and what to do when a storm is near. Always remember, the best way to stay safe is to plan ahead and be prepared.

Keep Learning and Sharing

The more you know about lightning safety, the better

equipped you are to help keep your family and friends safe. Share what you've learned today with others, and you'll help spread important safety tips that could save lives.

Remember, every thunderstorm brings a chance to observe one of the most spectacular shows nature has to offer. With the right knowledge and precautions, you can enjoy the majesty of the storm while staying safe and secure. Keep your curiosity sparked, and stay tuned for more weather wisdom and adventures!

5 /
the science of storms

how do thunderstorms develop?

HELLO, young storm watchers! Have you ever sat at a window and watched a thunderstorm brewing in the sky? It's like watching a live science show right above us. Thunderstorms are fascinating, and today, we're going to discover exactly how these powerful weather events develop. Strap in—it's going to be an electrifying ride!

What Makes a Thunderstorm?

Thunderstorms form from the same basic ingredients that make up any weather: moisture, unstable air, and lift. But for thunderstorms, these ingredients mix in just the right way to create something powerful and often spectacular.

1. Moisture: This is the water vapor in the air. For a thunderstorm to develop, there needs to be plenty of moisture, especially at lower levels of the atmosphere. This moisture is what feeds the clouds.

2. Unstable Air: Air becomes unstable when it's warmer than the air around it. Warm air rises, and if it rises fast enough, it can start to form a thunderstorm.

3. Lift: Something must lift the warm, moist air up into the atmosphere. This could be the heat from the sun warming the ground, a mountain range that air flows

over and rises, or a front where two different air masses meet and the warmer air is pushed up.

The Stages of a Thunderstorm

Thunderstorms go through three main stages during their life cycle: the developing stage, the mature stage, and the dissipating stage. Let's walk through these stages:

1. The Developing Stage

It starts with the sun warming the Earth's surface, and the air above it. The more the day heats up, the more the heat causes all of that moisture at the Earth's surface to start to evaporate and rise. The moist air keeps rising and the higher it gets, the cooler it becomes.

The cooling causes some of the water in the air to become a liquid and it becomes a cloud. This cloud can start off small—tiny, even! Think the fluffy cumulus clouds on a sunny day! But, the cloud can keep on going… if the conditions are right.

If there's enough moisture, instability and lift, the cloud can grow larger and larger and taller and taller, extending into higher, colder parts of the atmosphere. Now, this towering cloud is called a cumulonimbus cloud and believe it or not, this is the first sign that a big thunderstorm may be coming soon!

2. The Mature Stage

This is the main event! The mature stage is when the thunderstorm is strongest. As the cloud rises and cools, the water droplets inside the cloud join together and get heavier. Eventually, they become too heavy to stay in the cloud and start falling as precipitation—rain, hail, or sometimes snow if it's cold enough.

As these droplets fall, they drag down the air around them. This creates a downdraft—a rapid downward rush of cool air. At the same time, warm air continues to rise in an updraft. This battle between the updrafts and downdrafts is what drives the thunderstorm.

Lightning and thunder are also most intense during this stage. Lightning occurs because of the build-up of electrical charges in the cloud, and thunder is the sound made by the rapid expansion of air heated by the lightning. It's a noisy, wet, and wild phase!

3. The Dissipating Stage

Eventually, the thunderstorm starts to lose its punch. The downdrafts begin to overtake the updrafts, cutting off the warm air that fuels the storm. Without this fuel, the storm starts to weaken. The cloud may spread out, the rain lightens up, and the lightning and thunder stop.

As the storm calms, the cloud begins to break up and the sky clears. The thunderstorm dissipates, leaving cooler temperatures and often a fresh, clean smell in the air from a chemical released by the rain called petrichor.

Why Understanding Thunderstorms Matters

Understanding how thunderstorms develop not only helps us appreciate these powerful natural events but also teaches us how to be prepared. Knowing the signs of a developing storm can help us find shelter before it hits, keeping us safe from lightning, hail, and heavy rain.

Keep Watching and Learning

Every thunderstorm is a little different, and there's always more to learn from them. By paying attention to the weather around you and noticing the changes in the sky, you can become a junior meteorologist in your own right—predicting when a storm will arrive and knowing what it might bring.

the role of temperature, air, and moisture

Weather Wizards: Unpacking the Secrets of Temperature, Air, and Moisture

Now, let's explore the roles of temperature, air, and moisture in shaping the weather around us. These three elements are like the main ingredients in a recipe for weather. By understanding how they interact, you'll get a clearer picture of how storms, sunny days, and all sorts of weather patterns come to life.

The Magic of Temperature

Temperature is a measure of how hot or cold the air is, and it plays a massive role in the weather. You can think of temperature as the weather's mood setter. Here's why temperature is so crucial:

- Sun's Influence: The sun heats up the Earth's surface every day, and different surfaces—like water, sand, soil, and concrete—absorb and release heat at different rates. This creates different air temperatures, which can influence local weather patterns.

- Air Movements: Warm air rises and cool air sinks. When the sun heats the earth, it warms the air above it. This warm air rises because it's lighter than cool air. As it rises, it cools down, and the moisture it carries can form clouds and, eventually, precipitation. This process is called convection and is a key player in creating thunderstorms and many other types of weather.

- Highs and Lows: Temperature differences can lead to areas of high and low pressure. High-pressure areas usually bring clear skies and calm weather, while low-pressure areas can lead to storms and rain. This happens because air moves from high-pressure areas to low-pressure areas, and as it moves, it can bring different weather conditions with it.

The Power of Air

Air is our atmosphere, the layer of gases that surrounds the Earth. Without it, there would be no weather! Air affects the weather in several ways:

- Wind: Air in motion is what we feel as wind. Winds can be gentle or strong enough to form hurricanes. Wind is created by air moving from high-pressure areas to low-pressure areas. The greater the difference in pressure, the stronger the wind.

- Carrying Capacity: Air can carry things like moisture, heat, and pollutants. The ability of air to carry water vapor is especially important for weather. Warm air can hold more water vapor than cold air. When there's a lot of moisture in the air and the temperature drops, the moisture can condense into droplets, forming clouds and precipitation.

The Role of Moisture

Moisture refers to the amount of water vapor in the air. Without moisture, there would be no clouds, rain, snow, or ice—none of the fun stuff that makes weather interesting!

- Cloud Formation: As we mentioned earlier, when warm air rises and cools, the water vapor in the air can condense into tiny droplets, forming clouds. Different temperatures and amounts of moisture will create different types of clouds, which can tell meteorologists a lot about the weather to come.

- Rain and Snow: For precipitation to form, you need clouds that are full of moisture. When the droplets in clouds combine and grow too heavy to stay aloft, they fall to the ground as precipitation—rain, snow, sleet, or hail—depending on the temperature.

- Humidity and Comfort: Moisture in the air also affects how comfortable you feel. High humidity can make hot days feel hotter and sticky. That's because moist air makes it harder for sweat to evaporate off your skin, which is how your body cools itself down.

Bringing It All Together

so if you think of yourself as a bit like a weather detective, and you are trying to solve the mystery of what tomorrow's weather is going to be like, you would look at some clues. these clues would include how warm or cool the air will be for example (temperature), what the air would be doing (is the air moving? is it rising? is it falling?), and how wet it is (does the air contain a lot or a little moisture?). by understanding the clues you can work out whether or not you should take an umbrella with you to protect you from the rain or sunglasses to help you to see on a very sunny day.

introduction to other storm-related phenomena (hail, gusts)

Hello, young weather explorers! Have you ever been curious about the other exciting phenomena that often accompany thunderstorms, like hail and gusts of wind?

Well, you're in for a treat today as we delve into these fascinating aspects of stormy weather. Just like detectives, we'll uncover the secrets behind these powerful elements and see how they fit into the bigger picture of weather patterns.

Hail: The Frozen Wonder

Hail might seem like just hardened pieces of ice, but there's a lot more to it! Hail forms inside thunderstorms when updrafts (which are strong currents of rising air) carry raindrops upwards into extremely cold areas of the atmosphere. These raindrops then freeze into balls of ice. As more water freezes onto the surface of these balls, they grow larger and larger.

1. How Hail Forms: Think of a thunderstorm like a giant ice-making machine. Inside this machine, updrafts act like powerful elevators, lifting droplets of water high into the storm where it's below freezing. Here, the droplets turn into small ice pellets. If the updraft is strong enough, it will keep pushing these pellets up into the storm, where layers of water freeze over them, again and again, making them grow bigger until they're too heavy for the updraft to support. Then, they fall to the ground as hailstones.

2. Sizes and Damage: Hail can vary in size from tiny pebbles to as big as a grapefruit. The size of hail depends largely on the strength of the updrafts in the thunderstorm. Larger hailstones can cause a lot of damage to

cars, roofs, and crops. That's why hailstorms are taken very seriously, especially in places known as "Hail Alley" in the United States, where these storms are more common.

Gusts: The Sudden Blasts

Gusts are sudden, brief increases in the speed of the wind, often occurring during storms. They are like the bursts of energy that storms sometimes throw at us. Gusts can be quite powerful and dramatic, capable of knocking over trees and power lines, and even turning a calm day into a chaotic one within seconds.

1. How Gusts Form: Gusts generally happen when cold air from a thunderstorm cloud rushes downwards and hits the ground, spreading out quickly in all directions. This is called a downdraft. When this cold, dense air hits the ground, it has nowhere to go but sideways, creating a gust front. This is the sharp increase in wind that you feel before a storm arrives.

2. The Power of Gusts: While gusts can be exciting, they can also be dangerous. They can disrupt outdoor activities and cause damage to structures. High winds can turn unsecured objects into flying debris, which is why it's important to secure loose items like patio furniture before a storm hits.

Understanding These Phenomena

Both hail and gusts are important to meteorologists (scientists who study the weather) because they can help predict other weather conditions and warn people about potential dangers. By studying how and when hail forms and how gusts behave, meteorologists can provide better forecasts and warnings, which help keep everyone safer.

Keep Learning and Exploring

Each storm brings a new opportunity to observe and learn more about the incredible forces of nature. With your newfound knowledge about hail and gusts, you can watch storms with an understanding of what's happening when these phenomena occur. Keep a journal of the storms you observe and note down any hail or strong wind gusts you experience. This can be a fun way to track your observations and see how much you've learned.

6 /
famous lightning strikes

historical accounts of famous lightning strikes

1. The Kite Experiment of Benjamin Franklin (1752)

One of the most famous lightning stories involves Benjamin Franklin, one of America's Founding Fathers, who was also a curious scientist. Franklin was intrigued by lightning and wanted to prove that it was a form of electricity. During a thunderstorm in 1752, Franklin flew a kite with a metal key attached to the string. When lightning struck the kite, the electric charge flowed down the string and gave him a shock. This daring experiment led to the invention of the lightning rod, which protects buildings from lightning damage by directing the electricity safely into the ground.

2. The Tower of St. Nazaire (1915)

During World War I, the Tower of St. Nazaire in France was hit by lightning. This might sound like just another lightning strike, but what happened next was extraordinary. The tower had been used to store ammunition, and the lightning caused a massive explosion that destroyed the tower and caused significant damage to the surrounding area. This event showed just how powerful and destructive lightning could be when it interacted with human-made structures, especially those containing explosive materials.

3. The Destruction of the Space Shuttle Challenger (1986)

While lightning did not directly strike the Space Shuttle Challenger, concerns about lightning led to a critical decision that would have historical implications. On the day of the launch, there were fears of lightning from anvil clouds, which can extend many miles from a thunderstorm's core. Although lightning didn't strike, the decision to launch in such cold weather, partly influenced by the need to avoid possible future lightning storms, contributed to the shuttle's tragic explosion shortly after liftoff. This highlighted the importance of understanding weather conditions in the planning of space missions.

4. Roy Sullivan, the Human Lightning Rod

Roy Sullivan, a U.S. Park Ranger, earned a place in the Guinness Book of World Records as the person struck by lightning the most times—seven! Between 1942 and 1977, Sullivan was struck by lightning multiple times in various situations, surviving all of them. His story is almost unbelievable and reminds us of the random and powerful nature of lightning. Sullivan's experiences have helped to raise awareness about lightning safety and the importance of taking cover during thunderstorms.

5. Lightning Strikes the Statue of Liberty

The Statue of Liberty, located in New York Harbor, is struck by lightning multiple times each year due to its prominent position and metal structure. These strikes are powerful reminders of why tall structures need lightning rods. The Statue of Liberty itself acts as a gigantic lightning rod, safely directing the electrical currents away from the structure and its visitors, ensuring that this symbol of freedom and democracy stands unharmed by nature's forces.

Learning from Lightning

These stories show us not just the dangers of lightning, but also how much we have learned from observing and studying this powerful natural phenomenon. Each lightning strike tells a story of energy, power, and sometimes, the intersection of human activity with nature's forces.

interesting facts about lightning

1. Lightning is Faster Than You Think!

Lightning can travel at about 270,000 miles per hour! That's way faster than a racecar, faster even than sound itself. In fact, that's why we see lightning flash before we hear the thunder. If you're watching a storm, count the seconds between seeing lightning and hearing thunder. Every five seconds equals about one mile distance from the storm. This little trick is called the "flash to bang" method.

2. A Single Bolt Can Light Up a Town

A typical lightning bolt can carry up to one billion volts of electricity. To put that in perspective, it only takes about 120 volts to light up a standard light bulb in your home. Imagine how many bulbs you could light with a single lightning bolt!

3. Lightning Doesn't Only Strike the Tallest Buildings

It's a common myth that lightning only strikes the tallest buildings. While it's true that tall, pointy objects are more likely to get hit, lightning can strike anywhere, even in open fields. The Empire State Building, for instance, gets struck by lightning about 23 times a year because it's so tall and well, pointy. But lightning can also strike the ground right next to it!

4. Lightning Strikes the Same Place More Than Once

One of the most shocking facts about lightning is that it can strike the same place not just twice, but many times. The Empire State Building's frequent lightning strikes are a perfect example. There's no truth to the old saying that lightning never strikes the same place twice. In fact, it seems to like some places quite a bit!

5. Positive and Negative Lightning Bolts

Most lightning bolts carry a negative charge, but there is such a thing as positive lightning, which is much rarer and even more dangerous. Positive lightning bolts come from the top of thunderclouds and can strike ground up to ten miles away from their cloud. They also pack a much bigger charge, which can be up to ten times stronger than a negative bolt. So, if you hear about a positive lightning strike, you know it's a big deal!

6. The Mystery of Ball Lightning

Ball lightning is one of the rarest and least understood forms of lightning. People who've seen it describe it as a floating, glowing sphere that can move through the air or even enter buildings through windows and doors. Scientists are still trying to figure out exactly what causes ball lightning and how it works, making it one of the most mysterious aspects of weather!

7. Lightning Helps the Planet

Lightning is not just a destroyer; it's also a creator. When it strikes, it can help break down nitrogen in the air. This nitrogen combines with other chemicals to create nitrates, which are a type of fertilizer that helps plants grow. So, in a way, lightning is nature's way of helping feed the Earth.

8. Lightning on Other Planets

Lightning isn't just an Earth thing; it happens on other planets, too! Scientists have observed lightning bolts on Jupiter and Saturn. Imagine what a storm would look like there!

9. The Color of Lightning

The color of a lightning bolt can tell you about the atmosphere where it formed. Lightning can appear white, blue, purple, and even green! The color depends on the type of dust and moisture in the air, which affects how the light is scattered.

10. Safe During a Storm

If you're indoors during a thunderstorm, stay off corded phones, computers, and other electrical equipment that put you in direct contact with electricity. And despite being a good conductor of electricity, cars are relatively safe from lightning because the metal frame of the vehicle can help direct the electricity to the ground.

fictitious stories of survival and safety

1. The Miraculous Survival of the Hiking Family

Imagine you're hiking with your family on a beautiful mountain trail when suddenly the sky darkens, and a storm rolls in. This is exactly what happened to the Martins, a family of four. As they hurried down the trail to find shelter, lightning struck a nearby tree, which exploded from the electrical charge. Splinters and sparks flew everywhere, but luckily, they remembered what to do.

The Martins crouched low to the ground in a group, making sure not to lie flat. They found a low spot away from trees and covered their ears to protect against the thunder. This quick thinking kept them safe, and although they were shaken, they were unharmed. This story reminds us that understanding and remembering safety tips can be life-saving.

2. The Fisherman and the Bolt from Above

Mr. Thomson, a seasoned fisherman, was out on the lake when a storm quickly approached. Knowing that water attracts lightning and that boats on open water are at high risk, he immediately headed for shore. But just before he could dock, a lightning bolt struck the water near his boat.

The electrical charge from the lightning bolt traveled through the water. Feeling a tingling sensation, Mr. Thomson lay down in the bottom of the boat, an act that potentially saved his life by minimizing his contact with conductive surfaces. He escaped with minor injuries and a big story about the power of nature. His experience shows us the importance of getting off the water quickly during a storm.

3. The Runner Who Outran Lightning

Julie was jogging in her neighborhood park, with earphones in, when a storm began. Initially, she didn't hear the thunder, but then she saw a flash of lightning. Remembering her safety training, she didn't head to the nearest tree for shelter or keep running in the open field. Instead, Julie sprinted to a community center nearby, which was her best option for safe shelter.

By the time she reached the center, the storm was directly overhead. Thanks to her quick response to seek proper shelter, Julie avoided what could have been a direct hit from lightning. This story highlights the importance of immediate action and why it's crucial to know your surroundings and the location of safe shelters.

4. The Boy Who Lived

Nine-year-old Aaron was playing in his backyard when a thunderstorm suddenly appeared. Not fully aware of the dangers of lightning, he started to run home but stopped under a large tree to avoid getting wet. Lightning struck the tree, and Aaron was thrown to the ground by the force of the resulting ground current.

Miraculously, he suffered only minor burns. Aaron's story became a lesson for his whole community about why trees are dangerous shelters during storms. This event led to a local campaign about lightning safety, teaching kids and adults alike to never take shelter under trees and always move indoors when a storm approaches.

5. The Golfers' Narrow Escape

A group of teenagers was playing golf when the sky turned threatening. The golf course, full of metal clubs and open spaces, is one of the riskiest places to be during a lightning storm. As soon as they heard the first rumble of thunder, they dropped their clubs and ran to the safety of the clubhouse.

One bolt of lightning struck a tree right next to the 18th hole just minutes after they left the area. The teens' prompt decision to leave their game and seek safety undoubtedly saved them from severe injuries. This tale serves as a powerful reminder that fun and games must always take a backseat to safety.

Learning from Lightning

Each of these stories teaches us crucial lessons about respecting the power of storms and knowing how to act quickly and correctly to stay safe. Lightning is a fascinating but dangerous element of nature, and understanding how to protect ourselves ensures that we can enjoy the beauty of storms without putting ourselves at risk.

experiments and activities

safe, simple experiments to understand static electricity

DID you ever wonder why you get a little shock when you slide down a slide? Or why you shock your family after walking across a carpeted room? How about when your hair stands up after taking off a wool hat on a dry winter day? These phenomena are all related to static electricity. So, today, we're going to learn more about it, and do a few fun experiments to better understand it! Let's become static electricity experts!

What Is Static Electricity?

Static electricity is the build-up of electric charge on the surface of objects. It happens when certain materials rub against each other, like your shoes on the carpet or a balloon on your hair. The friction causes electrons (tiny particles that carry electric charges) to move from one object to another. This leaves one object with extra electrons (making it negatively charged) and the other with fewer electrons (making it positively charged). When objects with opposite charges come close, they attract each other—zap!

Experiment 1: Magic Balloon

• • •

Materials Needed:

- A balloon

- Your hair or a wool sweater

- A wall (or other flat surfaces that can attract the balloon)

Instructions:

1. Inflate the balloon and tie the end to keep the air inside.

2. Rub the balloon vigorously against your hair or the wool sweater for about 30 seconds to a minute. What you're doing here is transferring electrons from your hair or the sweater to the balloon, giving the balloon a negative charge.

3. Slowly bring the balloon near a wall. Watch as the balloon sticks to the wall all by itself! This happens because the negatively charged balloon induces a positive charge on the wall's surface, causing the two to attract.

What's Happening?

The balloon sticks to the wall because of the attraction between the negatively charged balloon and the positively charged wall. This shows how static electricity can cause objects to attract each other.

Experiment 2: Dancing Paper

Materials Needed:

- Small pieces of paper (like confetti or punched-out paper holes)
- A plastic comb
- A wool sweater or your hair

Instructions:

1. Cut or punch small pieces of paper and place them on a table.

2. Take the plastic comb and run it through your hair or rub it on the wool sweater for about a minute to charge it up.

3. Hold the comb close to the pieces of paper without touching them. Watch as the paper pieces start to move toward the comb and even jump up to stick to it!

What's Happening?

By rubbing the comb on your hair or sweater, you're

giving the comb a negative charge. The small paper pieces, which are positively charged, are attracted to the negatively charged comb. This experiment shows how static electricity can make objects move or jump.

Experiment 3: Water Bender

Materials Needed:
- A plastic comb
- A thin stream of water from a faucet

Instructions:
1. Charge the comb by running it through your hair or rubbing it against a sweater as you did in the previous experiments.
2. Carefully bring the comb near a thin stream of water (be careful not to touch the water with the comb).
3. Watch as the water stream bends toward the comb!

What's Happening?
When you bring the charged comb near the water, the negative charge of the comb attracts the positive charges in the water molecules, causing the water to bend

towards the comb. This fascinating effect shows how even a liquid's direction can be influenced by static electricity.

Why These Experiments Matter

These experiments are not just fun tricks; they help us understand the basic principles of electricity. By exploring how static electricity works, you can learn about the forces that hold atoms and molecules together and how materials can interact through electrical charges.

diy weather station: tools kids can make at home to observe weather

Have you ever wanted to predict the weather just like the experts on TV? Or maybe you're curious about how weather works and want to observe it up close? Well, you're in luck because today we're going to learn how to make your very own weather station right at home, using simple tools and materials. Let's dive into the exciting world of DIY meteorology and start our journey to becoming backyard weather experts!

· · ·

Why Build a Weather Station?

Building a DIY weather station is not only a super fun project, but it also helps you learn more about the environment and how different weather conditions are measured. By observing the weather yourself, you'll get a hands-on understanding of concepts like temperature, wind speed, and rainfall, which are essential for predicting the weather.

Tools You'll Need for Your Weather Station

Here are some basic instruments you can make and what they measure:

1. Thermometer (Temperature): Measures how hot or cold the air is.

2. Rain Gauge (Rainfall): Measures how much rain has fallen.

3. Wind Vane (Wind Direction): Shows the direction the wind is coming from.

4. Anemometer (Wind Speed): Measures how fast the wind is blowing.

5. Barometer (Air Pressure): Measures the pressure in the atmosphere, helping to predict weather changes.

Let's get started on how to create each one!

1. Making a Thermometer

While making a true thermometer at home can be tricky because it involves chemicals like mercury or alcohol, you can create a simple version that demonstrates the principle of thermal expansion and contraction using just a few household items.

Materials:
- Clear plastic bottle
- Water
- Rubbing alcohol
- Food coloring
- Clear plastic straw
- Modeling clay

Instructions:

1. Fill the plastic bottle halfway with equal parts of water and rubbing alcohol.

2. Add a few drops of food coloring and mix.

3. Put the straw in the bottle, making sure it does not touch the bottom.

4. Use the modeling clay to seal the mouth of the bottle around the straw but make sure the straw is still open at the top.

5. As the air inside the bottle heats up or cools down, the liquid mixture will expand or contract, moving up or down the straw. This won't give you exact temperature readings, but you can observe how changes in temperature affect the liquid level.

2. Crafting a Rain Gauge

A rain gauge is one of the simplest weather tools you can make, and it's fantastic for measuring how much rain falls over a period.

Materials:

- Large measuring cup or any container with straight sides
- Ruler

- Permanent marker

Instructions:

1. Place the ruler inside the container.

2. Use the permanent marker to mark off each centimeter or inch on the container.

3. Place the gauge outside in an open area when you expect rain.

4. After the rain, check how high the water has reached to see how much rain has fallen.

3. Building a Wind Vane

A wind vane helps you determine the direction the wind is blowing from, which is crucial for understanding weather patterns.

Materials:

- Sturdy cardboard
- Pencil with an eraser on top
- Straight pin
- Plastic drinking straw
- Paper (to make an arrow)

- Compass

Instructions:

1. Cut an arrow shape out of the cardboard and attach it to one end of the straw.

2. Push the pin through the middle of the straw and into the pencil eraser, allowing the straw to rotate freely.

3. Use the compass to align your wind vane with the cardinal directions.

4. Place your wind vane outside and observe the direction the arrow points when the wind blows.

4. Assembling an Anemometer

An anemometer measures wind speed. Here's how to make a simple one:

Materials:
- 4 small paper cups
- 2 straws
- Pin
- Pencil with an eraser on top
- Stapler

. . .

Instructions:

1. Cross the straws and staple them together to form an 'X.'

2. Attach a cup to each end of the straw segments, making sure they all face the same direction.

3. Push the pin through the center of the crossed straws and into the pencil eraser.

4. Place the anemometer outside. The wind will catch the cups, causing it to spin. The faster it spins, the stronger the wind is blowing.

5. Creating a Barometer

Making a simple barometer to measure changes in air pressure is a great way to predict weather changes.

Materials:

- Empty can
- Balloon
- Rubber band
- Straw
- Index card

. . .

Instructions:

1. Cut the balloon and stretch it over

the open end of the can.

2. Secure it with a rubber band.

3. Tape one end of the straw to the center of the balloon.

4. Set the can on a flat surface and tape the index card behind it so the straw points at the card.

5. Mark the position of the straw on the card. Changes in air pressure will make the balloon stretch or contract, moving the straw up or down. This movement can help you predict if the weather is likely to be stormy or clear.

Becoming a Junior Meteorologist

With these tools, you've got your very own weather station! Keep a weather journal to record your observations. Note the temperature, wind direction, how much rain falls, and any changes in air pressure you notice. Over time, you'll start to see patterns and become a real expert in your local weather.

activity sheets (puzzles, coloring pages of lightning, etc.)

After learning all about weather and how to make your own weather station, it's time to add some extra fun to your journey into meteorology. This chapter is all about activity sheets, puzzles, and coloring pages that not only make learning about weather super enjoyable but also help you remember what you've learned in a creative way. So, grab your pencils, crayons, and thinking caps— it's time to play and learn!

Why Activity Sheets?

Activity sheets are a fantastic way to reinforce what you've learned through hands-on experiences. They can help you visualize different weather phenomena, understand complex ideas like air pressure and humidity, and improve your memory and problem-solving skills. Plus, they're just plain fun!

Types of Activity Sheets

. . .

1. Coloring Pages: These aren't just for little kids! Coloring can be relaxing and educational for explorers of all ages. You'll find pages featuring thunderstorms, the water cycle, different types of clouds, and even famous lightning strikes. As you color, try to remember key facts about each phenomenon.

2. Word Searches: Find hidden weather terms in a grid of letters. This helps you get familiar with the vocabulary of meteorology. For example, you might search for words like "cumulus," "stratus," "barometer," or "anemometer." Each word you find will be a piece of the weather puzzle.

3. Crossword Puzzles: These puzzles will challenge you to remember what you've learned. For example, the clue might be "The instrument used to measure wind speed," and the answer would be "anemometer." This is a great way to test your knowledge and learn new facts.

4. Mazes: Navigate your way through a maze to escape a hurricane or find your way to a weather station. Mazes

help improve your problem-solving skills and can teach you about the paths of storms or the flow of ocean currents that affect weather.

5. Connect-the-Dots: These sheets will reveal hidden pictures related to weather, such as a lightning bolt, a tornado, or a snowflake. As you connect each dot, you'll see the magic of complex weather patterns come to life right before your eyes.

6. DIY Weather Diary: Keep track of the weather each day with your DIY weather diary. Draw pictures of what the sky looks like, jot down temperatures, or record how much rain fell. Over time, you'll have a personal weather book that shows you how the weather changes throughout the year.

How to Use Your Activity Sheets

1. Educational Tool: Use these sheets during your study time to make learning more interactive. For example, after reading about hurricanes, complete a puzzle or coloring page about hurricanes to reinforce what you've

learned.

2. Family Fun Time: Bring your family together and challenge them with a weather crossword puzzle or work on a weather-related art project. It's a great way to share what you've learned and spend quality time with loved ones.

3. Rainy Day Activities: What's better than studying weather while watching it? On rainy or snowy days, pull out your activity sheets and dive deep into weather study while the storm rages outside. It's the perfect weather lab right at your fingertips.

Creating Your Own Weather Art

Don't stop with the activity sheets provided! Try creating your own drawings or models of weather systems. You could draw your interpretation of the water cycle, craft a mobile of the solar system that includes the sun's effects on Earth's weather, or even build a model of a weather station with materials you find around the house.

· · ·

Sarah Michaels

Weather on Display

Consider creating a weather bulletin board in your room or a shared space in your home. You can display your completed activity sheets, your own weather drawings, and daily weather reports. This not only shows off your hard work but also helps you live the role of a young meteorologist.

8 /
the wonders of thunder and lightning

cultural significance of thunder and lightning in various cultures

HAVE you ever sat under a shelter during a storm, watching as the lightning illuminates the sky and the thunder crashes all around, and wondered if people in other parts of the world see it the way you do? Thunder and lightning have been part of every culture's mythology, history, and holy celebrations. Throughout history, these sights and sounds have been a signal of divine activity, a sign of something coming, and a source of both fear and awe. In this article, we will take a trip around the world to discover how different cultures see the same thing.

Thunder and Lightning in Mythology

Many cultures see thunder and lightning as powerful symbols. Often, these natural phenomena are associated with gods and goddesses of the sky and storms. Here are a few examples:

1. Zeus - Ancient Greece

- In Greek mythology, Zeus is the king of the gods, and he wields lightning as his weapon. The Greeks believed that when Zeus was angry, he would throw lightning bolts crafted by the Cyclopes. This was not only a way to explain the powerful, sometimes destructive nature of storms but also reflected Zeus's role as a god who maintained order and justice.

2. Thor - Norse Mythology

- Thor, the Norse god of thunder, is perhaps one of the most famous storm-related deities. Armed with his enchanted hammer Mjölnir, which could produce lightning, Thor was said to protect Asgard and Midgard (the world of humans) from giants and monsters. Every thunderstorm was seen as Thor riding through the heavens, battling the forces of chaos.

3. Raijin - Japan

- In Japanese folklore, Raijin is the god of lightning, thunder, and storms. He is often depicted playing drums that create thunder. Raijin is considered a powerful and fearsome god, but also one who brings life-giving rain to crops. Farmers might revere Raijin, hoping that he would be generous in his rainfall but gentle with his storms.

4. Tlaloc - Aztec

- Tlaloc was an important deity in Aztec culture, associated with water, fertility, and storms. He controlled the rain, lightning, and thunderstorms, which were crucial for agriculture. The Aztecs held ceremonies and offered sacrifices to Tlaloc to ensure rain and protect their crops from destructive storms.

Thunder and Lightning in Folktales and Art

Thunder and lightning have also made their way into countless folktales and artistic expressions, often symbolizing human emotions such as anger, surprise, or divine intervention.

1. African Folktales

- In many African stories, thunder and lightning are seen as communications from ancestral spirits or gods. These stories often teach respect for nature and the power that it holds.

2. Native American Lore

- Different tribes have various interpretations of thunder and lightning. For example, the Navajo believed that the Thunderbirds, giant supernatural beings in the form of birds, created thunder and lightning. The flashes of lightning were the birds' eyes blinking, and the thunder was the flap of their wings.

Celebrations and Festivals

In some cultures, festivals celebrate the power and mystery of thunder and lightning, acknowledging their vital role in agriculture and the natural cycle of seasons.

1. India - Monsoon Festivals
   - In India, the arrival of the monsoon season brings festivals like Teej and Onam, where people give thanks for the rain and its life-sustaining properties, vital for the harvest. While not directly celebrating lightning, these festivals acknowledge the entire monsoon experience, of which thunder and lightning are dramatic parts.

2. Bali - Piodalan
   - This Balinese ceremony happens every 210 days to honor the gods associated with a particular temple. Part of the celebration includes acknowledgment of the

monsoon season, where thunder and lightning play key roles in the dramatic skies that characterize this period.

Learning from Legends

As you can see, thunder and lightning are more than just weather phenomena; they are a rich part of human culture and storytelling. From the mighty Thor to the fearful Raijin, each story or depiction helps us understand how humans across time and space have tried to make sense of the world around them.

lightning and thunder in literature and movies

Lightning and Thunder in Literature

Lightning and thunder have been used in literature not just as dramatic backdrops, but as pivotal elements that drive the plot or deepen the atmosphere of a scene. Here are a few notable examples:

1. "Macbeth" by William Shakespeare

- In Shakespeare's Macbeth, thunder and lightning open the play, setting a tone of ominous doom. The stormy weather accompanies the three witches, whose prophecy sets Macbeth on his tragic path. Here, Shakespeare uses the elements to foreshadow the turmoil and treachery that will unfold, intertwining nature's unrest with human conflict.

2. "Frankenstein" by Mary Shelley
- In this iconic novel, lightning plays a crucial role in bringing Frankenstein's monster to life. Victor Frankenstein harnesses the power of a lightning storm in his scientific experiment, leading to the creation of the novel's famous creature. Shelley's use of lightning symbolizes both enlightenment and destruction, highlighting the duality of human progress.

3. "The Storm" by Kate Chopin
- Chopin's short story uses a thunderstorm as a key element where the main characters reunite and their passions reignite, mirroring the storm's intensity. The storm outside reflects the storm of emotions inside, serving as a perfect metaphor for the characters' feelings.

· · ·

Sarah Michaels

Lightning and Thunder in Movies

In movies, lightning and thunder often heighten the tension or signify key moments. Their visual and auditory impact makes them powerful tools for filmmakers. Here are some instances where lightning and thunder significantly impact cinematic storytelling:

1. "Back to the Future" (1985)

- Lightning is central to the climax of this beloved sci-fi film. The protagonists must harness a lightning bolt to power their time-traveling DeLorean back to the future. The anticipation of the lightning strike creates a nail-biting sequence that remains one of the film's most memorable moments.

2. "The Shawshank Redemption" (1994)

- A pivotal scene in this film features thunder and lightning as Andy Dufresne escapes from prison. The thunder masks the sound of his hammer breaking through the sewer pipe, symbolizing a stroke of fate aiding his quest for freedom. The storm not only covers his escape but also cleanses him as he emerges free into the river.

. . .

3. "Thor" (Marvel Cinematic Universe)

- In the "Thor" movies, thunder and lightning are not just weather phenomena but are part of Thor's character, as he is the Norse god of thunder. The films use these elements to showcase his godly powers, often with visually stunning effects that enhance the action scenes.

Why Do Writers and Filmmakers Love Thunder and Lightning?

Thunder and lightning provide a sensory-rich experience. Visually, lightning illuminates scenes with a stark, dramatic flair, while the rumble of thunder adds a deep, resonant layer to the auditory landscape of a story. These elements can:

- Signify the presence of supernatural or divine powers.
- Enhance the mood of suspense, danger, or foreboding.
- Symbolize internal or external conflict.
- Propel the plot forward through specific, climactic events.

. . .

Creating Your Own Stormy Scenes

Now, why not try creating your own stormy scene? Imagine a story or a scene for a movie where lightning and thunder play a crucial role. Think about what they could represent in your story. Is it the anger of a character, a major revelation, or simply the perfect backdrop for a mysterious event?

how you can help at home during a thunderstorm

Thunderstorms can be exciting to watch, but they also require us to be prepared and safe. Did you know that even as a kid, you can play a big role in helping your family stay safe during a thunderstorm? Let's explore some important and fun ways you can contribute when those dark clouds roll in.

Understanding Thunderstorm Safety

First, it's great to understand why we need to be careful during thunderstorms. Thunderstorms can bring lightning, heavy rain, strong winds, hail, and sometimes even tornadoes. Each of these can be dangerous, so knowing what to do can help keep everyone safe.

1. Helping to Prepare an Emergency Kit

One of the best ways to prepare for any emergency, including thunderstorms, is to have an emergency kit ready. You can help your family by making sure your home's emergency kit is well-stocked and up-to-date. Here's what you can do:

- Gather Supplies: Help collect necessary items like batteries, a flashlight, a first-aid kit, water bottles, and non-perishable snacks. You can make a checklist and tick off each item as you add it to the kit.
   - Expiration Dates: Check the expiration dates on food and batteries. It's important to replace anything that's out of date.
   - Easy Access: Make sure the emergency kit is in a place where everyone in the family can easily find it. A good spot might be in the kitchen or near the front door.

2. Creating a Family Safety Plan

. . .

Being prepared means having a plan. You can help by working with your family to create a safety plan for different types of emergencies, including thunderstorms. Here's how you can get involved:

- Learn and Share: Learn the safety tips for thunderstorms, like staying away from windows, avoiding electrical appliances, and not using the shower during a storm. Then, share what you've learned with your family.
   - Practice Drills: Suggest having a family drill. Practice what to do and where to go in your house if a severe storm hits. This can make it easier to remember in case of a real emergency.

3. Monitoring the Weather

With a parent's help, you can learn how to use a weather app or website to keep an eye on the weather. Here's how you can be the family weather reporter:

. . .

- Weather Alerts: Learn to recognize weather alerts like severe thunderstorm warnings and watches. You can check the weather online and inform your family if a storm is coming.

- Teach Others: Show your siblings or friends how to use the weather app. It's more fun when you're learning together!

4. Securing Outdoor Items

Before a thunderstorm arrives, it's important to secure outdoor items that could blow away or get damaged. Here's what you can do:

- Bring in Toys: Make sure all your outdoor toys are brought inside or secured so they don't get blown away or damaged.

- Help with Furniture: Offer to help your parents bring in or secure outdoor furniture. This prevents them from being tossed around by strong winds, which could be dangerous.

5. Comforting Pets

. . .

Pets can get really scared during thunderstorms. You can be a big help by keeping them calm and safe. Here's how:

- Cozy Spaces: Help create a comfortable space for your pets. This could be a quiet corner with their favorite blanket or a special nook where they feel safe.

    - Stay Calm: Pets can sense when you're scared. By staying calm, you can help your pets feel calmer too.

glossary

definitions of key terms used in the book

1. Atmosphere
   - What It Is: The layer of gases that surrounds Earth. It's made up of layers, including the troposphere (where weather happens), the stratosphere, and others.
   - Why It Matters: The atmosphere protects us from the sun's harmful radiation and holds the air we need to breathe. It's also where all the weather action happens!

2. Barometer
   - What It Is: An instrument used to measure air pressure.
   - Why It Matters: Changes in air pressure can tell us about upcoming weather changes. A falling barometer

means bad weather is coming, while a rising barometer means the weather will likely improve.

3. Climate

- What It Is: The average weather conditions in a place over a long period, usually at least 30 years.

- Why It Matters: Knowing the climate of an area can help people prepare for typical weather patterns and understand what crops to plant or what clothes to wear across different seasons.

4. Condensation

- What It Is: The process by which water vapor in the air turns into liquid water.

- Why It Matters: Condensation is crucial for cloud formation and is part of the water cycle that supports life on Earth.

5. Humidity

- What It Is: The amount of water vapor present in the air.

- Why It Matters: Humidity affects how we perceive temperature. High humidity makes it feel hotter, while low humidity makes it feel cooler. It also influences weather patterns and precipitation.

6. Lightning

- What It Is: A sudden, visible discharge of electricity between cloud and ground, between clouds, or within a cloud.

- Why It Matters: Lightning is a powerful natural phenomenon that can cause fires and electrical outages. It's fascinating to study and important to respect for safety.

7. Meteorology

- What It Is: The science that deals with the atmosphere and its phenomena, including weather and climate.

- Why It Matters: Understanding meteorology helps us predict weather, prepare for storms, and even study climate changes impacting our planet.

8. Precipitation

- What It Is: Any form of water, liquid or solid, that falls from clouds and reaches the ground. This includes rain, snow, sleet, and hail.

- Why It Matters: Precipitation is crucial for providing the water needed by all living things. It also influences weather patterns and climate.

9. Thunder

- What It Is: The sound caused by the rapid expansion of air along the path of a lightning bolt.

- Why It Matters: Thunder helps us determine how far away a storm is, based on the time delay between seeing lightning and hearing thunder.

10. Tornado
    - What It Is: A violently rotating column of air touching the ground, usually attached to the base of a thunderstorm.
    - Why It Matters: Tornadoes can cause significant damage to structures, harm people, and disrupt communities, making it essential to study them for improved safety measures.

11. Weather
    - What It Is: The state of the atmosphere at any given time, including things like temperature, humidity, precipitation, cloudiness, visibility, and wind.
    - Why It Matters: Weather affects daily decisions, from what you wear to how you travel. Understanding weather helps us live more comfortably and safely.

12. Wind Vane
    - What It Is: A device that shows the direction from which the wind is blowing.
    - Why It Matters: Wind direction can tell us a lot about upcoming weather changes and is also crucial for activities like flying, sailing, and even farming.

resources

Websites for Weather Wizards

1. National Geographic Kids (kids.nationalgeo-graphic.com)

- Dive into the science of weather with interactive games, videos, and articles designed just for kids. Learn about everything from tornadoes to blizzards.

2. Weather Wiz Kids (weatherwizkids.com)

- Created by meteorologist Crystal Wicker, this website is dedicated to teaching kids about weather. It includes easy-to-understand explanations and fun experiments you can do at home.

3. NOAA's SciJinks (scijinks.gov)

- This site is all about weather and satellite meteorology. It's packed with games, stories, and activities that make learning about weather both fun and educational.

Videos That Make Weather Learning Fun

Sometimes, watching videos can be one of the best ways to learn, especially when it comes to something as visual as weather. Here are some great video resources:

1. "Bill Nye the Science Guy" on Weather
   - Check out episodes of Bill Nye's classic science show that focus on weather topics. Bill Nye makes learning about science super fun and engaging.

2. The Weather Channel Kids (weatherchannelkids.com)
   - This site offers videos that explore various weather phenomena in ways that are easy for kids to understand.

3. YouTube Edu Channels like CrashCourse Kids and SciShow Kids
   - These channels offer fantastic, short videos that explain weather patterns, the science behind them, and much more. They're perfect for a quick learning session.

Apps to Explore

In addition to books and websites, there are some great apps that can turn your tablet or smartphone into a mini weather station:

1. Weather by Tinybop

- This interactive app lets you play with and learn about different weather conditions. See how changing variables like temperature and wind affect a landscape!

2. NOAA Weather Radar Live & Alerts

- It's a bit more advanced, but this app lets you track real-time weather patterns just like professional meteorologists do.

meteorological societies and science museums

Why Visit Meteorological Societies and Science Museums?

Meteorological societies and science museums aren't just places to see cool stuff—they're also centers of learning where you can ask questions, participate in experiments, and maybe even meet experts who study the weather for a living! Here's what you can do:

1. See Real Weather Instruments: From giant radar dishes that can track storms to anemometers that measure wind speed, you'll get to see the tools that scientists use in real life.

2. Participate in Workshops and Camps: Many of these places offer special programs where you can learn more about weather through hands-on activities.

3. Meet Professional Meteorologists: Some events might feature talks or meet-and-greets with weather scientists, where you can learn about what it's like to chase storms or forecast weather.

Finding Meteorological Societies

Meteorological societies are groups where people who love weather, from amateur enthusiasts to professional meteorologists, come together to share knowledge and learn. Here's how you can find one near you:

1. Ask Your Science Teacher: They often know about local science clubs and societies and can point you in the right direction.

2. Check the Library: Your local library might have bulletin boards with information or even host meetings.

3. Search Online: Look up "meteorological society" or "weather club" along with the name of your town or

nearest city. Their websites might list event schedules, membership options, and contact information.

Visiting Science Museums

Science museums are treasure troves of knowledge, with exhibits on everything from the solar system to the deep sea, including lots of weather-related displays. Here's how to make the most of a visit:

1. Check for Special Exhibits: Many museums have temporary exhibits that focus on specific areas like weather and climate. These can be a great opportunity to learn something new.

2. Attend a Planetarium Show: If your local museum has a planetarium, check out shows about Earth's atmosphere and weather phenomena.

3. Explore Interactive Displays: Many science museums feature interactive weather stations where you can create your own weather forecast or see how different weather instruments work.

Example Contacts to Get You Started

While I can't list every local resource here, I can give you a few examples of places to look into for inspiration:

- The Exploratorium in San Francisco, CA: Known for its hands-on science exhibits, including many on weather and environmental science.

- The Franklin Institute in Philadelphia, PA: Offers a weather exhibit where you can learn about meteorology.

- The Museum of Science in Boston, MA: Features exhibits on lightning, clouds, and storm phenomena.

- Your Local University: Many universities have meteorology departments with outreach programs for kids. They might offer tours, lectures, or even weather camps.

Preparing for Your Visit

When you plan to visit a meteorological society or science museum, here are a few tips to get the most out of your experience:

- Prepare Questions: Think about what you're most curious about and prepare some questions in advance. This way, you won't forget what you wanted to ask.

- Bring a Notebook: Keep a journal of what you learn. You might want to jot down interesting facts or draw pictures of the exhibits you see.

- Follow Up: If you enjoyed your visit, consider becoming a member or signing up for a newsletter to stay connected with their events.

Milton Keynes UK
Ingram Content Group UK Ltd.
UKHW020350031224
452051UK00008B/247

9 798330 614059